Windsongs and Spindrifts

by

Pearl Newton Rook

DORRANCE PUBLISHING CO., INC.
PITTSBURGH, PENNSYLVANIA 15222

To my sister, Margaret N. Matthews.

ISBN # 0-8059-6127-5
Printed in the United States of America

First Printing

For information or to order additional books, please write:
Dorrance Publishing Co., Inc.
701 Smithfield Street
Pittsburgh, Pennsylvania 15222
U.S.A.
1-800-788-7654
Or visit our web site and on-line catalog at
www.dorrancepublishing.com

Contents

Other Books
by Pearl Newton Rook

Shifting Sands
   The Mitre Press, London, England, 1971

Hidden Universe
   Dorrance and Co., Philadelphia, Pennsylvania, 1974

The Sound of Thought
   (co-authored with husband, Douglas Lee Rook)
   Windy Row Press, Petersborough, New Hampshire 1977

Where Still the Source Endures
   The Golden Quill Press, Francestown, New Hampshire, 1986

   Awarded Golden Medallion, 1988, International
   Poetry Competition, Australia

In grateful acknowledgment to the editors and publishers of the follow-
ing publications in which these poems first appeared:

American Poet, Avalon Dispatch, Lake Effect,
Lake Oconee Living Magazine, North American
Mentor, Parnassus, Poet, The Poet's Touchstone,
Rhyme Time, Rochester Poets Anthology, World
Poet, U.S. Poets

Windsongs

Measure by measure, I hear
chinook and sirocco celebrate
meteor nights and rainbow days.
They play their special songs
among the leaves and harmonize
with the lake purling on summer shores.

I will keep that music singing
always in my mind, wherever I am,
even when the winds change and drums
of thunder strike their solemn beat
against the darkening sky.

Haiku

A fledgling seagull
lands on the bones of a barge
oops, lost his grip—splash

Evening

Sunset—
tangerine sky
eyes peeking through grey clouds
looking for a spirit to spook—
pumpkin

Thirteenth Moon

Evening, heavy with silence,
muffles everything, even my breath,
which might startle the leaves.
Far away, an owl hoots—
waits for an answer.
It is a long wait. Faintly again,
it's call haunts the woods.
When I hear the echo around me
I fly away into the night,
a shadow winging toward the moon.

Island Sanctuary

All year long, the Beach House
beside the willow tree and near
the shore beckons me to its site.
Here I can see the great heron
glide along rays of the morning sun
or listen to the owl's grace note
question the evening air. Despite
the spider's lace curtains across
the windows or the nest a mouse
left behind the door, I come
to take my place within these walls.
Here, my heart-thoughts beat in harmony
with island symphonies of wave
and wind. Here the magic of love wraps
my spirit within its mystic sphere.

Encounter

Beneath the locust tree in fading light
the cottage waits for me beside the lake.
Inside, I ask the ghosties to ignite
and scare the shadows forth for goodness' sake.

I need to search the corners, under beds,
behind the doors, for spirits who can spell
the magic words to bring celestial heads
to keep me safe within its fragile shell.

In place of angels chorusing a hymn
a mischief maker comes for me instead
and weaves a spider's net too strong and thin
for me to see it or rewind its thread.

A thought unfurls: I will the night to ebb
and day to come to exorcise the web.

Strength

Flowers
small, white petals
bloom before winter ends—
the withered heart also unfolds—
snow-drops

Spring Break

Ice flow
soft, glistening
crinkles against the shore
fairy wind chimes, peaceful, buoyant
crystals

For a Rainy Day

Catch a singing moment,
hold it in your heart,
keep it for another time,
when dreams fall apart.

Rare Gem

Bluebird
royal watchet
flying before our startled eyes—
wing-crafted song of happiness
whistler

Whatever You Do

Be careful where you walk,
for the ground trembles and troubles
the turf. Better to soft-step along
the path that deer and fox use,
where the earth accepts
all travelers quietly.

Be careful, too, what you say,
for you may frighten flowers,
birds, and even the stars
should you speak of extinction.

Better to sing a melody
to quicken the essence
of all creatures
wherever they are.

Weapon

Pencil in hand, she thinks
until words escape from lead
to find a way of their own
into the mind of others.
It writes more than she knows;
she sees more than it can tell.

The pencil, stubby, almost useless,
erases a thought. She wonders
what it will do next. Poised
above paper, it still has a sharp
point and she is still thinking.

By Word of Mouth

They come wherever a group
gathers to cultivate a new culture.
The disease, common to personalities
bored with a lifestyle unbefitting
their virus of careless chatter,
contaminates the air and spreads
with epidemic swiftness to others.
The canker, ingrown, is diagnosed
as "boob-onic" plague of the mind and mouth.

Wild Flowers

In the field of my thoughts,
imperfect deeds flourish
and spread like burdocks,
threatening my well being.
I weed such faults and transplant
them to paper with my pencil.
The list grows as each thought
clones another, until
furrows of failure line the page.

Near a pine grove in the woods
behind the house, I shred
the ledger into a hole.
A fox, with an arrow buried
in the heart of his brisket,
marks the grave of my guilts
and nudges the meadow of my mind
to sow seeds of a gentler design.

Eleanore's World

Just a daydream ago,
when I was yesterday's child,
my grandparents lived
but a field away, a magic field
where blackberry bushes—
my knights of the hedge—
protected my secret kingdom
against all, save for Cinderella's mice.
In that make-believe realm,
I made and wore a crown
of Queen Anne's Lace and nodded
to the buttercups and columbines—
my ladies in-waiting,
who in answer to a whimsy of wind
would, in turn, bow to me
as I swept along the path
to my tree-stump throne.

But the meadow days
are of another time;
my enchanted kingdom
was transformed into a house
where now, as mistress, I walk
its silent halls and still
hold court, where once
The flowers played, just a daydream ago.

Path Finder

Even with an atlas that shows
the way from one province
to another, I am lost. The sun rises
south of east and sets north of west
as the earth wobbles and I wander
the dirt roads of yesterday.

Then, descending from a ridge
lengthwise of a hill, into a valley
and around a lazy curve, I find
the family tree. Familiar as leaves
in a photograph album, the landmark
signifies the place where
my real journey begins.

Until I reached the end of the road
I did not realize I had traveled
for such a long time,
that I was homesick and might not
find the way back to tomorrow.

Summer Heat

Lightning
ribbon, streamer
strikes the mantle of earth.
Fear rumbles, courage knots, worry
signal

Birds

Seagulls
laughing clown birds
touch down on ice for lunch
skittish and chary scavengers
airlings

As the Sun Sets

Tree shadows yawn
across the cove to stretch
along the naked beach.
Leaves recite nursery rhymes
while wind and waves sing
a duet to lull the restless
evening into night.
But it is the litany of loons
that soothes the sleepless to dream,
as the personality of the day
fades from the face of the world.

Haiku I

Candle flame teases
moth to dance like a gypsy
poof! wings disappear

Haiku II

Red-winged blackbirds leaf
the birch for morning caucus
chill wind blows—tree hushed

Above and Beyond

So many times we sit on the tranquil terrace
and drink a toast to the view: rainbow wide,
galaxy high and as long as the tail
of a comet. At other times when so much
space terrifies the mind, we seek
the world that the porch affords. This place
where only wind and rain intrude, where
vision narrows, and sight sieves through
screens. And if the weather blacks out
the hours, we step through the threshold
of shelter and start a fire. Housebound,
we find the view unlimited from a plane
within ourselves that is ours alone.

Flight

Herons
flying phantoms
stir the morning mist aloft
soundless wonders; peaceful, patient
fishermen

Autumn

Fog bank
drumlin fashioned
eclipses the mainland shore.
Content, the hermit contemplates
the mist

Distractions

The wind is down, but waves
cannot resist the urge to break
on shore, trailing lace metaphors
in their wake; nor can the seagulls
refuse to fly on unseen currents of air
as flights of thought vanish
from your mind. In the distance,
similies drift like leaves
from a saffron cottonwood that hints
of an autumn to come. Nearby
small birds fight at the feeder.
Your words scatter like seeds
across the pages of a yellow pad—
brain food of a special kind?

A Pause in Time

While the sun waits to shine,
time also hesitates to start the day
and gives fog an interval
to find its way to shore. On the ridge
of a barrier beach, a leaf crashes
to the ground, a pile of debris heaves
a sigh. What is this place
where so intensified, you seem to float?
If you wait to move, will you vanish
in the morning mist?

Camp of the Winds

Without wind, the leaves and lake
have nothing to say. In the strange
silence, I laugh and talk about
the weather to fill the emptiness
of sound. But not for long.
The leaves and lake speak again—
louder and louder, day after day,
until I curse so much noise,
so much air in motion. The storm takes
the words out of my mouth to filter
a few among the trees, bounce others
across the water. After the tempest
swallows my demand to leave,
I yield to the wind, the leaves,
and the lake, because they are too busy
saying it all to listen to me.

Spindrift

Cobblestones, like dear old friends, once
new to the neighborhood, begin to wash
away with the spindrift of waves to another
beach. Then there are these trees
who have stood beside me for years.
I find a warmth in their wood
not found in the heart of stones.

Island Families

When out of sorts, they pass me by, eyes down
in search of friendship stones. What blades of grass
are there, do not exist. Beyond the mound
the path winds out of sight. A deep crevasse
awaits their aimless steps. Instead, they seek
the beach, companionship to while away
the afternoon in idle fun. A week
slips by. They feel less joy as day by day
the season slides toward fall and lack of light
allows the leaves to die along the lane
they need to find for peace of mind. Tonight
their waking dreams remember once again
the time when all was well by summer's end;
each one content to be his neighbor's friend.

Tyrant

The caitiff begins
as a mean little kid
playing games with currents
and tides. Growing stronger,
rougher, and higher, his head
swells, becomes a rogue wave.
The monster roars toward shore
to test his power, only to choke
and self-destruct
after "binge-ing" on the beach.

Foundling Moon

Cast off from Cygnus aeons ago,
I pinwheeled around the heavens
for centuries; peeked in dark holes
of space seeking sanctuary.
When the flames abandoned me
I was wrapped in a blanket
of gravity and left on the doorstep
of Earth, who adopted me. Now,
still tied to her apron strings,
lulled for so long in silent orbit
where even the stones have ceased
to rattle, I plod my obedient way.

I grow tired of wearing hand-me-downs
from a distant relative. Hidden
beneath my cover of primal dust,
deep in the subsoil of my being,
there lingers yet a wish and endless
desire for a light of my very own.

Jet Pilot

He leans forward
against mogul clouds
as he traverses
the slope of sky.

After he disappears
beyond a horizon hill
I become aware
of the shadow
his trail leaves behind.

Ritual

Because of Queen Anne's Lace
the clouds are grounded. Because
of chicory, the sky is, too.

They wait for the sun
to join them
because of leaves.

The Bay

Water
deep, land-locked bay
breeze wrinkles the surface
stirs dainty mythical thought waves
ichor

Threads

Spider
creepy crawler
spins a lace-curtain web
fragile symmetry sustains life
weaver

Conflagration

Fire sneaks, innocently, across
the ground to slip through cracks
in a wall and find a grate
warming left-over embers. Tongues
of flame lick the plate and wind,
still hungry from a diet of soot,
serves a full-course dinner
until the last crumbs of memories,
carried on a tray of heat waves,
are swallowed by the atmosphere.

Visitors

A pair
of troubadours
arrive and warm our hearth with song,
then leave to play among
the stones

Haiku

October wind rakes
clouds, heaps them aloft. Sunset
torches every pile

Dress Rehearsal

Quickly, child, take a seat
on the shore and watch
the spotlight catch the tree tops
unaware; see it turn the bay
into a diamond field.
Now look at the clouds—
like hand puppets
they rise above the footlights
of the horizon to speak
with the voice of thunder,
dance to the tune of windpipes,
and exit on cue to the south.

Yes, Megan, we will stay
for the second act,
when fall upstages summer—
and the third act, when the curtain
opens on winter's scene.

After intermission, we will applaud
for an encore until spring performs again.

Fragile Friendships

All summer long, the trees
wave and flutter in the wind,
greeting everyone. They speak
to each other and wish
a human being would say hello.
Autumn approaches. Wind,
out of control, blows their leaves
to the ground like friends
departing, who drop their calling
cards on the lawn. The air, in motion,
sends them aloft to land in my lap.
Too late, really, for me to cherish
the treasure they once were.

Happening in the Night

Spook house, perched like a teepee
above winged sumac, frightens day
into night, to hide in its shadow.
Phantom breeze calls an owl
to roost nearby. The ghost invites
them in. They speak in tongues,
mindful of others who prowl
the darkness looking for prey.
When dawn stalks the meadow,
spook and owl be-twitch themselves
into silence and thin air. They wait
and watch until the evening star
signals it is time for another
happening to begin in the night.

Costume Party

Now that most of the gypsies
have left the hills and woods
in broad daylight, the spooks
and spirits come by to clothe
the trees in grey. Pines collect
and put on display blond wigs
of poplar-leaf design, competing
with willows, who change their make-up
to a sunny disguise. In the fire bush
and sumac, gremlins and goblins
materialize as cottonwoods
spin fat buds for a home-spun
costume when spring arrives.

Decorators Incorporated

She slept, and he, impatient
with the ides of December
and moving water, waited
for the half-moon to rise
in the brittle sky
before he began to freeze
sound into silence.
After the marble light rimed
the rim of a cloud, he sent
the wind away while he feathered
ice across the lake. Pleased,
he frosted the weeds on the beach,
hung chandeliers on vines and trees.
Satisfied with his handiwork,
he hibernated. She roused
and, chilled to the bone, invited
the ice to thin into tinkling days,
prompted the wind to teach the waves
to purl on shore again, the weeds
to sing a new song. She persuaded
the vines and trees to replace
the crystals one by one
with emeralds. She knew
the Old Man would wake up
soon enough and re-decorate
as he stormed around the countryside.

Mountaintop

My words waste in the wind.
Idle questions fade faster
than thought ebbing to nothingness.
After night cloaks the day, stars
become old friends. Convinced
that I was not alone, I relaxed.

The mountain was born before time,
in the impersonal patience
of centuries, under a sun
that blazed from azure emptiness.

Stranded on this peak, black holes
of snow swallow my memories.

Endnote

Watching the hawk glide
you see his wingtips
touch the snow-covered field,
scattering dust that glistens
in the face of the morning sun.
As he snatches a song
in midair, a whole note
drifts to the ground. You shiver
when the shadow that waits
for all of us flies overhead.

Blizzard

Sumacs muffle their hands
in mittens, and willows
wrap themselves in scarves,
while bushes pull their caps
down to the ground. Meanwhile
the cottonwood buds grow fat
just waiting to unbutton
winter's coat in spring.

Lake Storm

This evening we saddle
the fireplace with wood.
As nervous flames stir
upward, we bridle fear,
give free rein to courage.
Wild horses race the wind
outside our door. They rear
and paw the darkness.
Morning finds a white
stallion stabled and still.

Time Lapse

The circadian clock signaled once,
awakening you with decent grace
to wonder what important thing
you knew last night. And then
you forgot to remember, as the time
between then and now became
a moment's notice later.

When evening came, you found
the years were thrust upon
the recent thoughts of dawn.
Yet the decades were lit
with a mellow lamp and now
leave you thinking and at peace
within the cupola of your mind.